GRAPHIC BIOGRAPHIES

ELIZABETH BLACKWELL

America's First Woman Doctor

by Trina Robbins

illustrated by Cynthia Martin
and Anne Timmons

Consultant:

Wendy Kline, Associate Professor

Department of History

University of Cincinnati

Capstone
press®

Mankato, Minnesota

Graphic Library is published by Capstone Press,
1710 Roe Crest Drive, North Mankato, Minnesota 56003.
www.capstonepub.com

Library of Congress Cataloging-in-Publication Data
Robbins, Trina.
    Elizabeth Blackwell: America's first woman doctor / by Trina Robbins; illustrated by
Cynthia Martin and Anne Timmons.
    p. cm.—(Graphic library. Graphic biographies)
    Summary: "In graphic novel format, tells the story of Elizabeth Blackwell, the first woman
to earn a medical degree in the United States"—Provided by publisher.
    Includes bibliographical references and index.
    ISBN-13: 978-0-7368-6497-8 (hardcover)
    ISBN-10: 0-7368-6497-0 (hardcover)
    ISBN-13: 978-0-7368-9660-3 (softcover pbk.)
    ISBN-10: 0-7368-9660-0 (softcover pbk.)
    1. Blackwell, Elizabeth, 1821–1910—Juvenile literature. 2. Women physicians—United
States—Biography—Juvenile literature. 3. Women physicians—England—Biography—Juvenile
literature. I. Martin, Cynthia, 1961– II. Timmons, Anne. III. Title. IV. Series.
R154.B623R58 2007
610.92—dc22   2006007802

Designer
Alison Thiele

Colorist
Matt Webb

Editor
Martha E. H. Rustad

Editor's note: Direct quotations from primary sources are indicated by a yellow background.

Direct quotations appear on the following pages:
Pages 8 (top), 12, 16, and 20, from *Pioneer Work in Opening the Medical Profession to Women* by
    Elizabeth Blackwell. Amherst, N.Y.: Humanity Books, 2005.

Printed in the United States   5426

TABLE OF CONTENTS

Chapter 1

A Dream Is Born

In the early 1800s, most girls did not go to school. Elizabeth Blackwell and her eight brothers and sisters were tutored at home. Their wealthy father believed girls should be educated as well as boys.

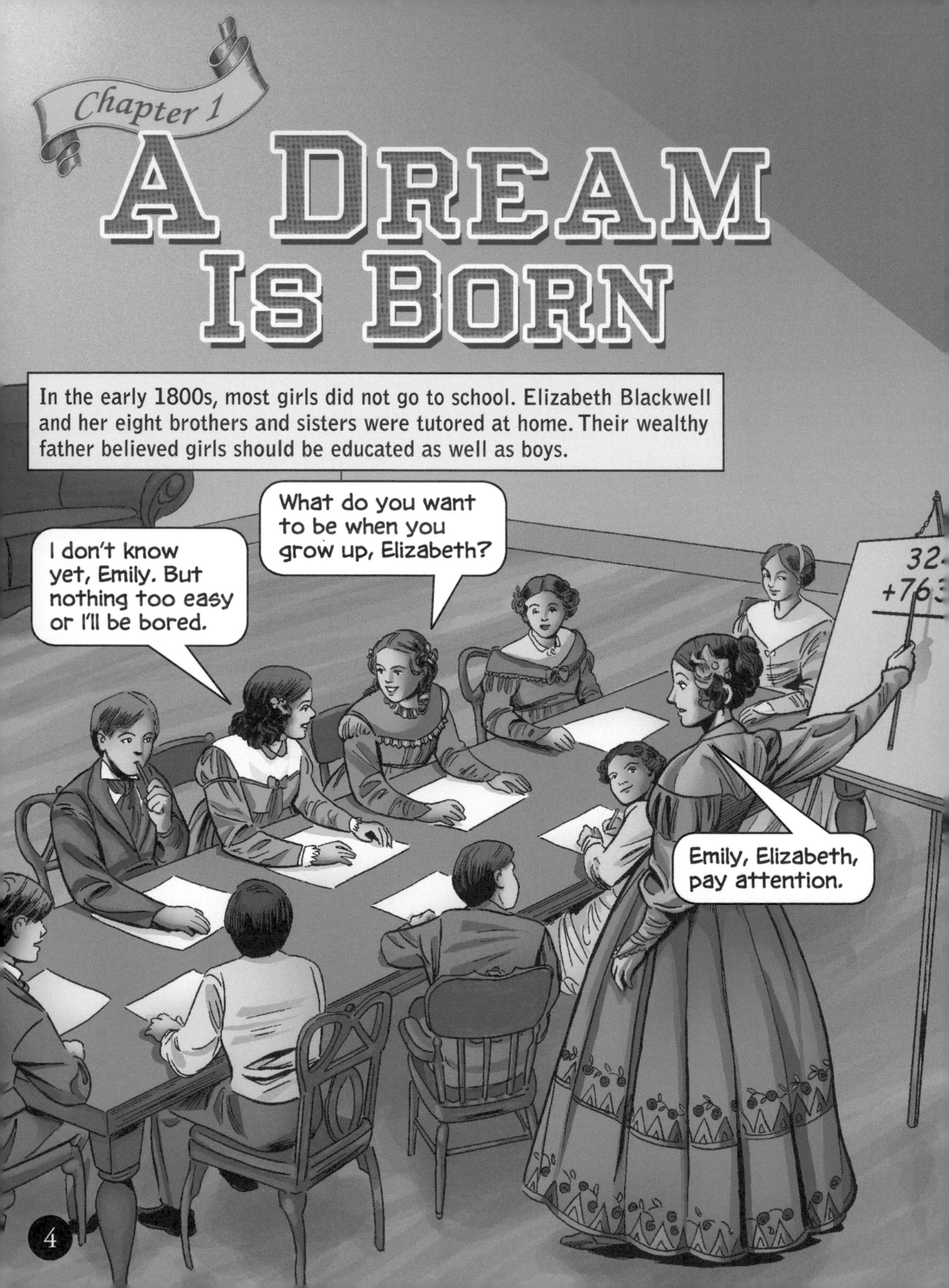
What do you want to be when you grow up, Elizabeth?
I don't know yet, Emily. But nothing too easy or I'll be bored.
Emily, Elizabeth, pay attention.

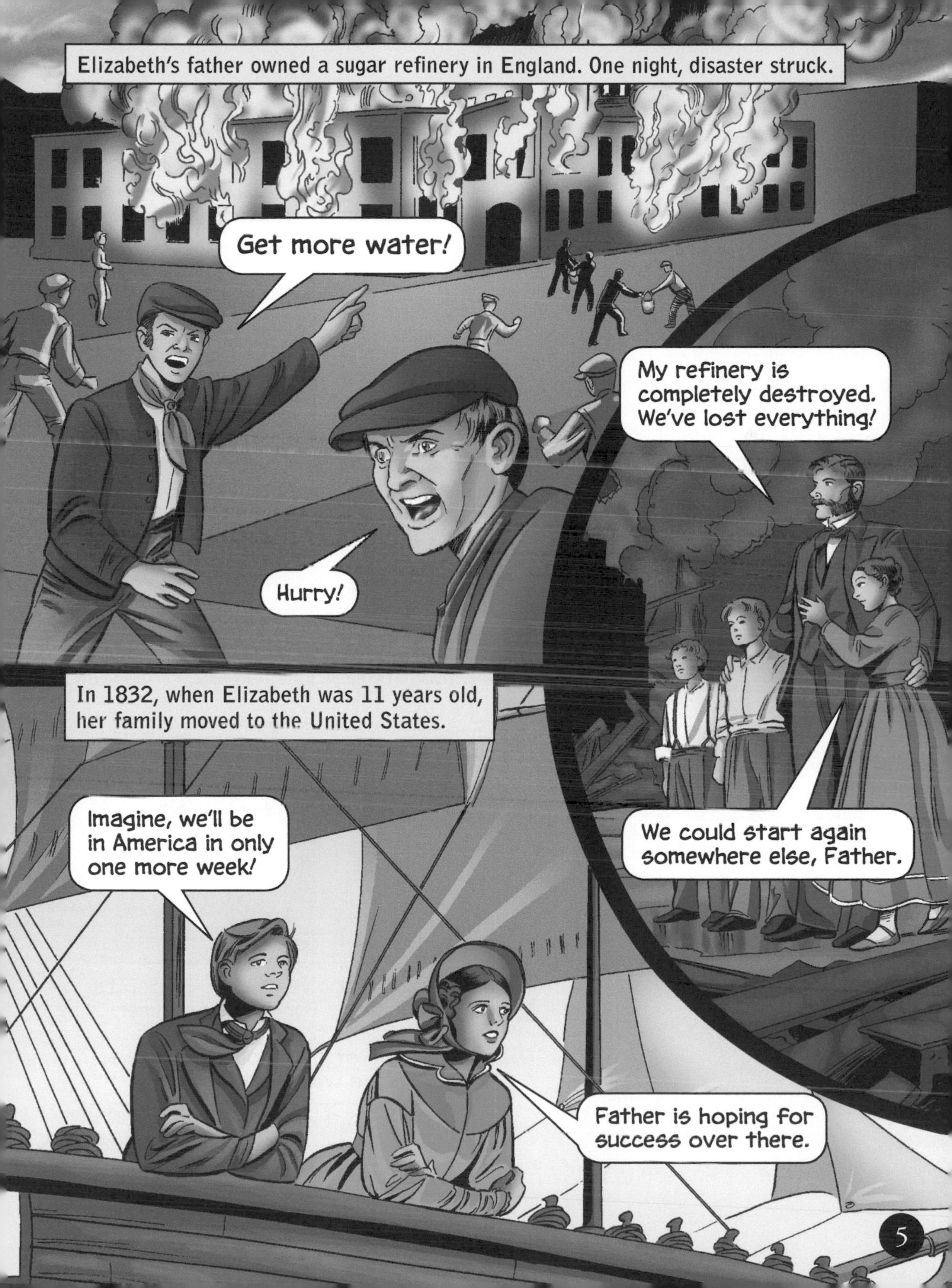

Elizabeth's father owned a sugar refinery in England. One night, disaster struck.
Get more water!
Hurry!
My refinery is completely destroyed. We've lost everything!
We could start again somewhere else, Father.
In 1832, when Elizabeth was 11 years old, her family moved to the United States.
Imagine, we'll be in America in only one more week!
Father is hoping for success over there.

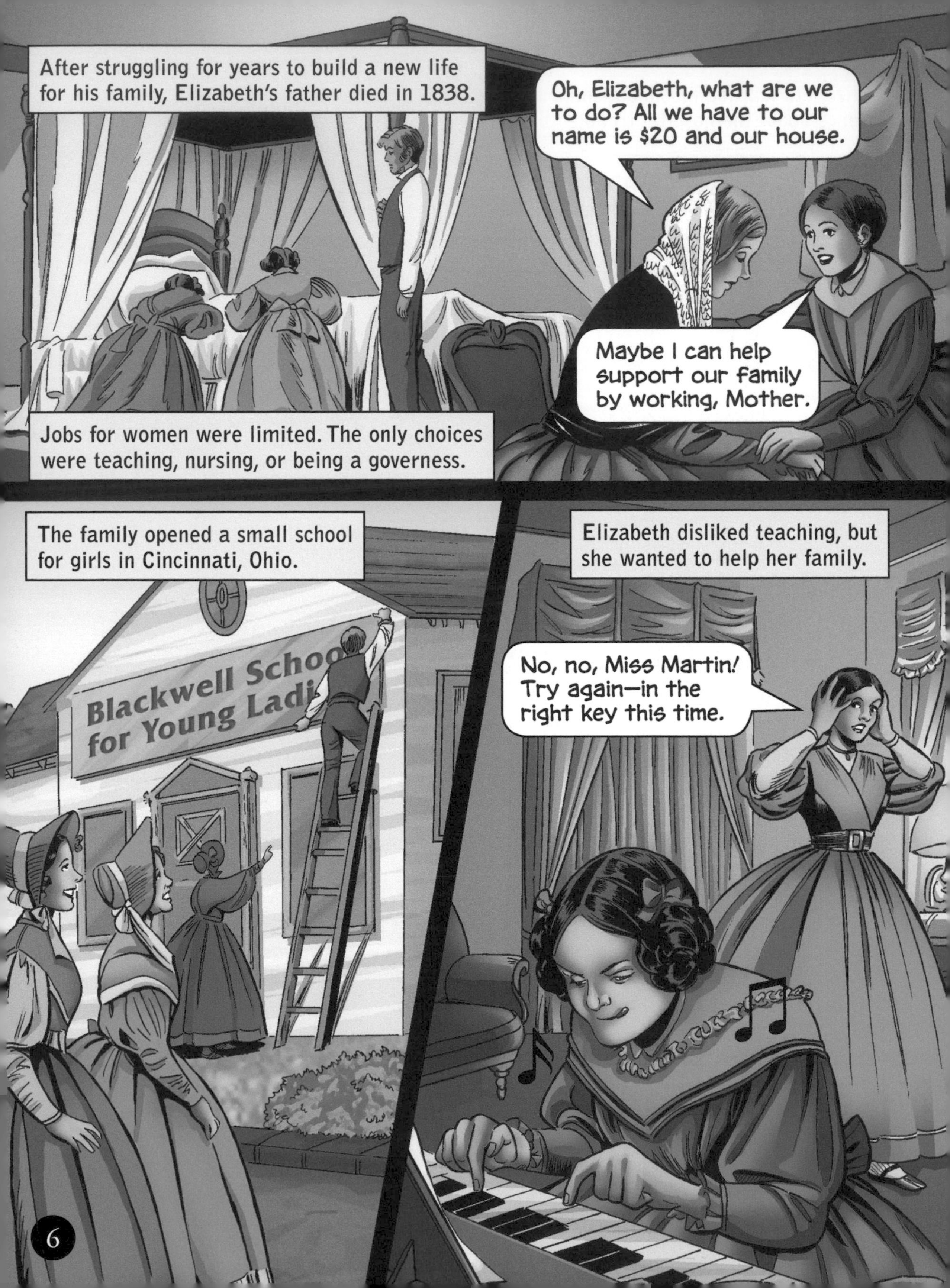
After struggling for years to build a new life for his family, Elizabeth's father died in 1838.
Oh, Elizabeth, what are we to do? All we have to our name is $20 and our house.
Maybe I can help support our family by working, Mother.
Jobs for women were limited. The only choices were teaching, nursing, or being a governess.
The family opened a small school for girls in Cincinnati, Ohio.
Blackwell Schoo
for Young Ladi
Elizabeth disliked teaching, but she wanted to help her family.
No, no, Miss Martin! Try again—in the right key this time.

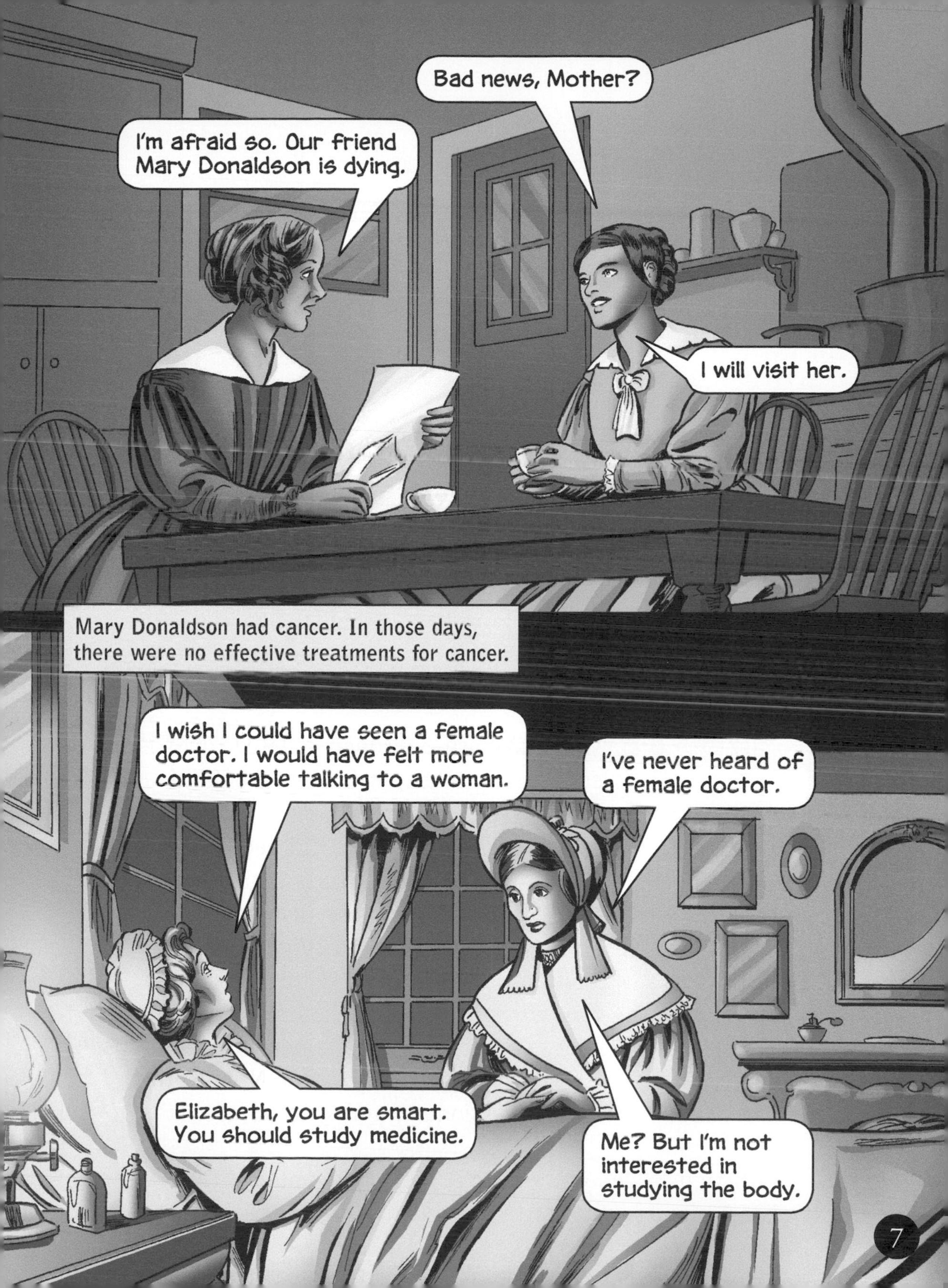

I'm afraid so. Our friend Mary Donaldson is dying.
Bad news, Mother?
I will visit her.
Mary Donaldson had cancer. In those days, there were no effective treatments for cancer.
I wish I could have seen a female doctor. I would have felt more comfortable talking to a woman.
I've never heard of a female doctor.
Elizabeth, you are smart. You should study medicine.
Me? But I'm not interested in studying the body.

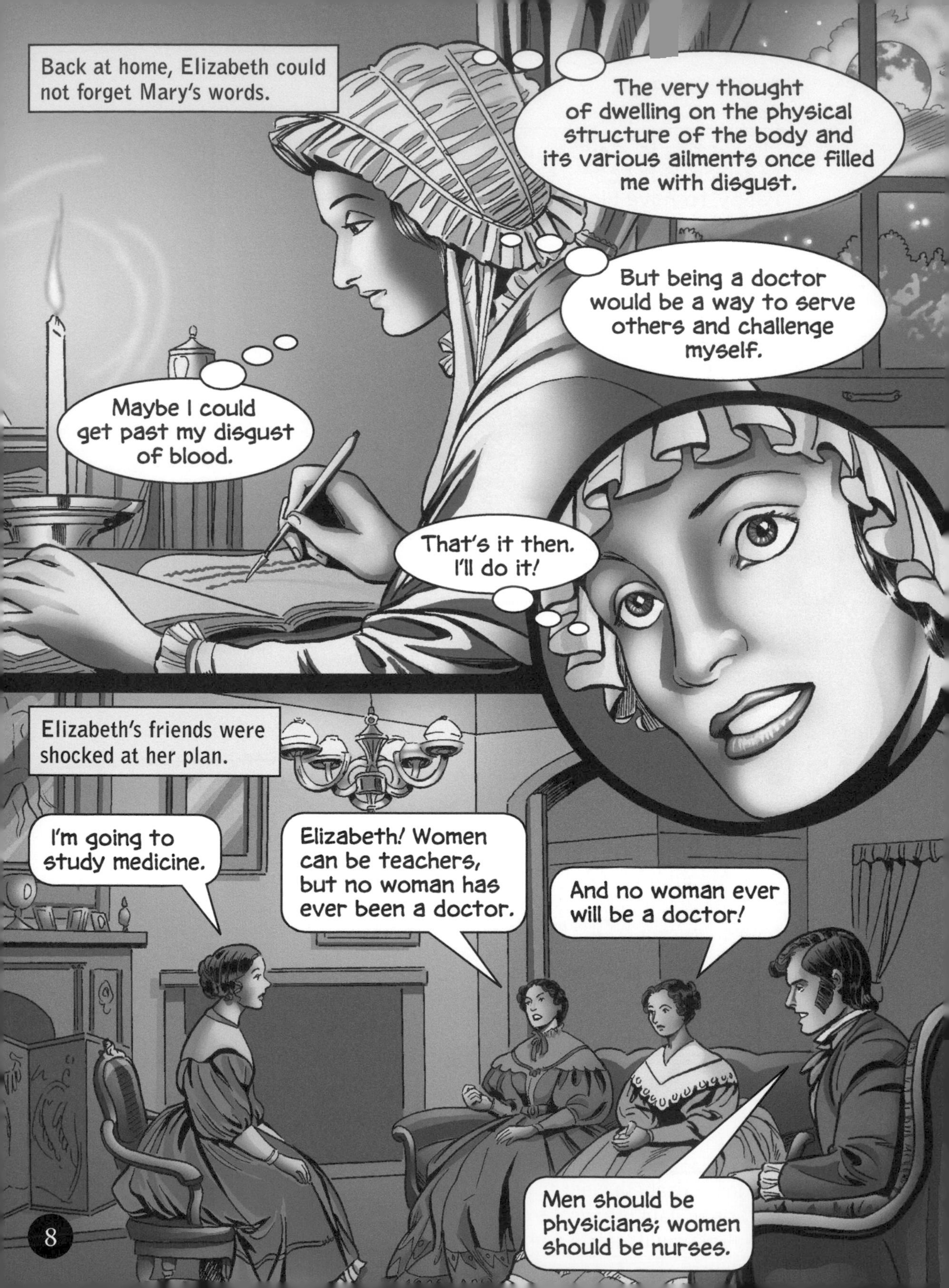
Back at home, Elizabeth could not forget Mary's words.
The very thought of dwelling on the physical structure of the body and its various ailments once filled me with disgust.
But being a doctor would be a way to serve others and challenge myself.
Maybe I could get past my disgust of blood.
That's it then. I'll do it!
Elizabeth's friends were shocked at her plan.
I'm going to study medicine.
Elizabeth! Women can be teachers, but no woman has ever been a doctor.
And no woman ever will be a doctor!
Men should be physicians; women should be nurses.

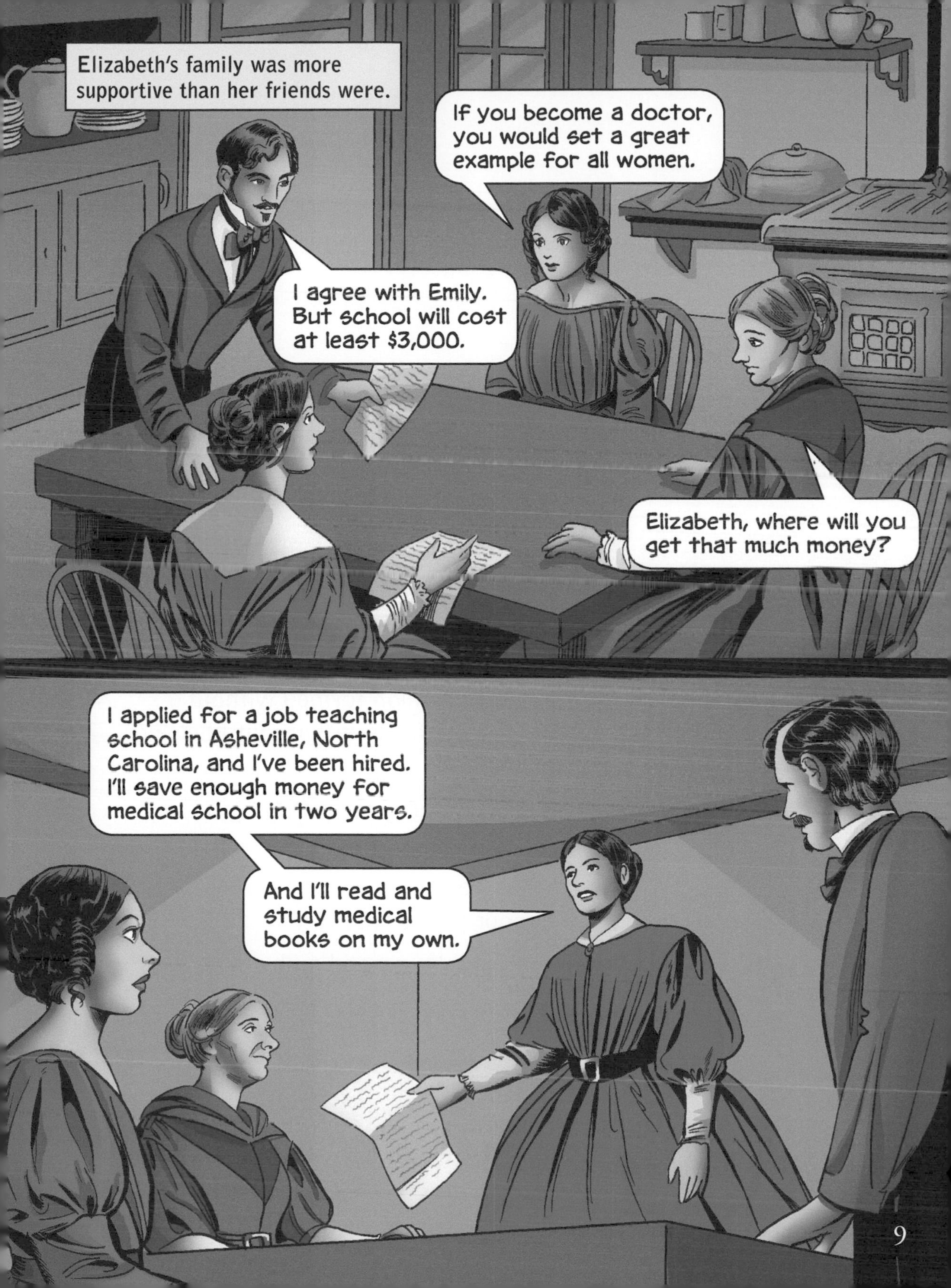
Elizabeth's family was more supportive than her friends were.
If you become a doctor, you would set a great example for all women.
I agree with Emily. But school will cost at least $3,000.
Elizabeth, where will you get that much money?
I applied for a job teaching school in Asheville, North Carolina, and I've been hired. I'll save enough money for medical school in two years.
And I'll read and study medical books on my own.

Chapter 2
Studying Medicine

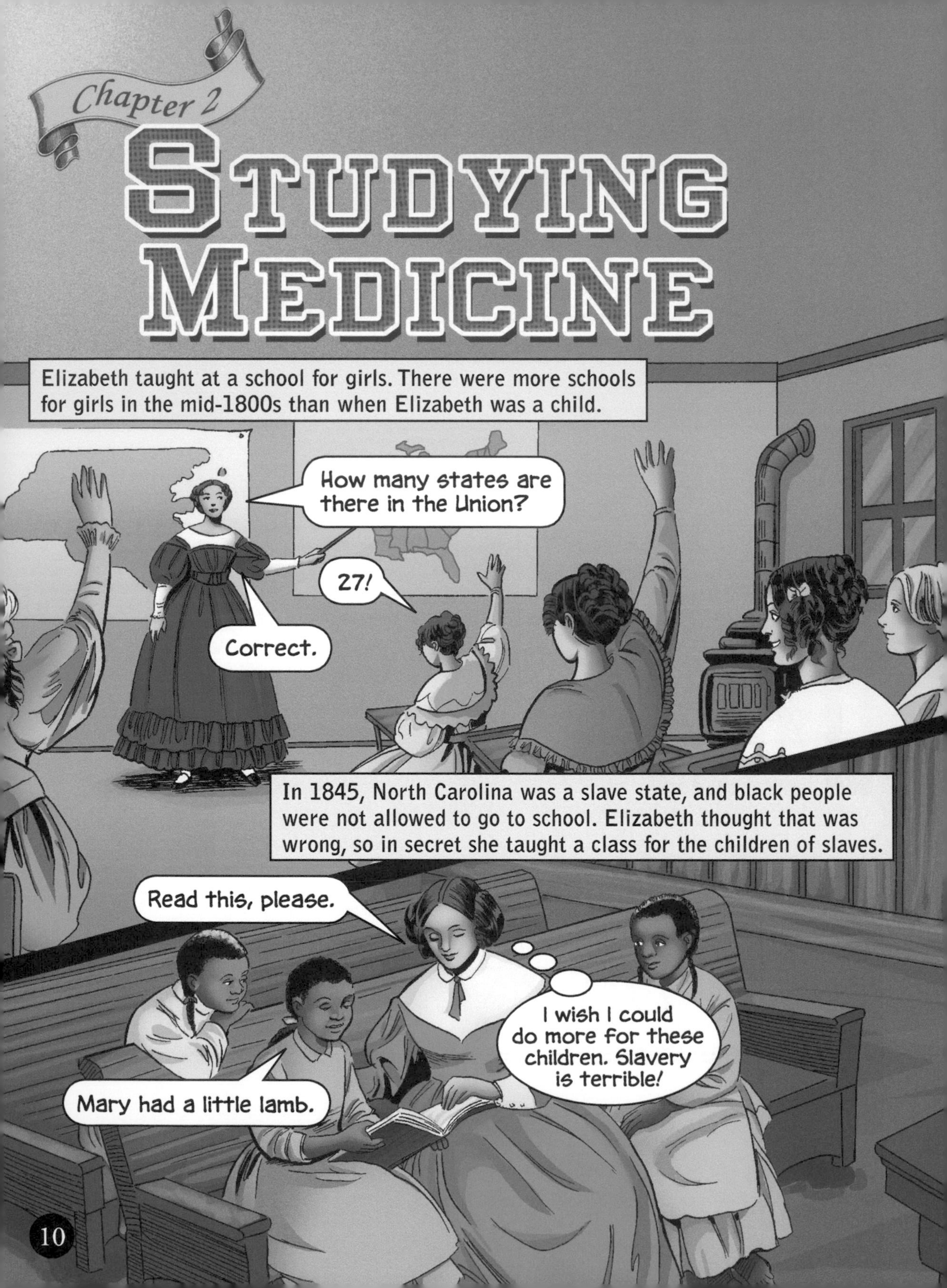
Elizabeth taught at a school for girls. There were more schools for girls in the mid-1800s than when Elizabeth was a child.
How many states are there in the Union?
27!
Correct.
In 1845, North Carolina was a slave state, and black people were not allowed to go to school. Elizabeth thought that was wrong, so in secret she taught a class for the children of slaves.
Read this, please.
Mary had a little lamb.
I wish I could do more for these children. Slavery is terrible!

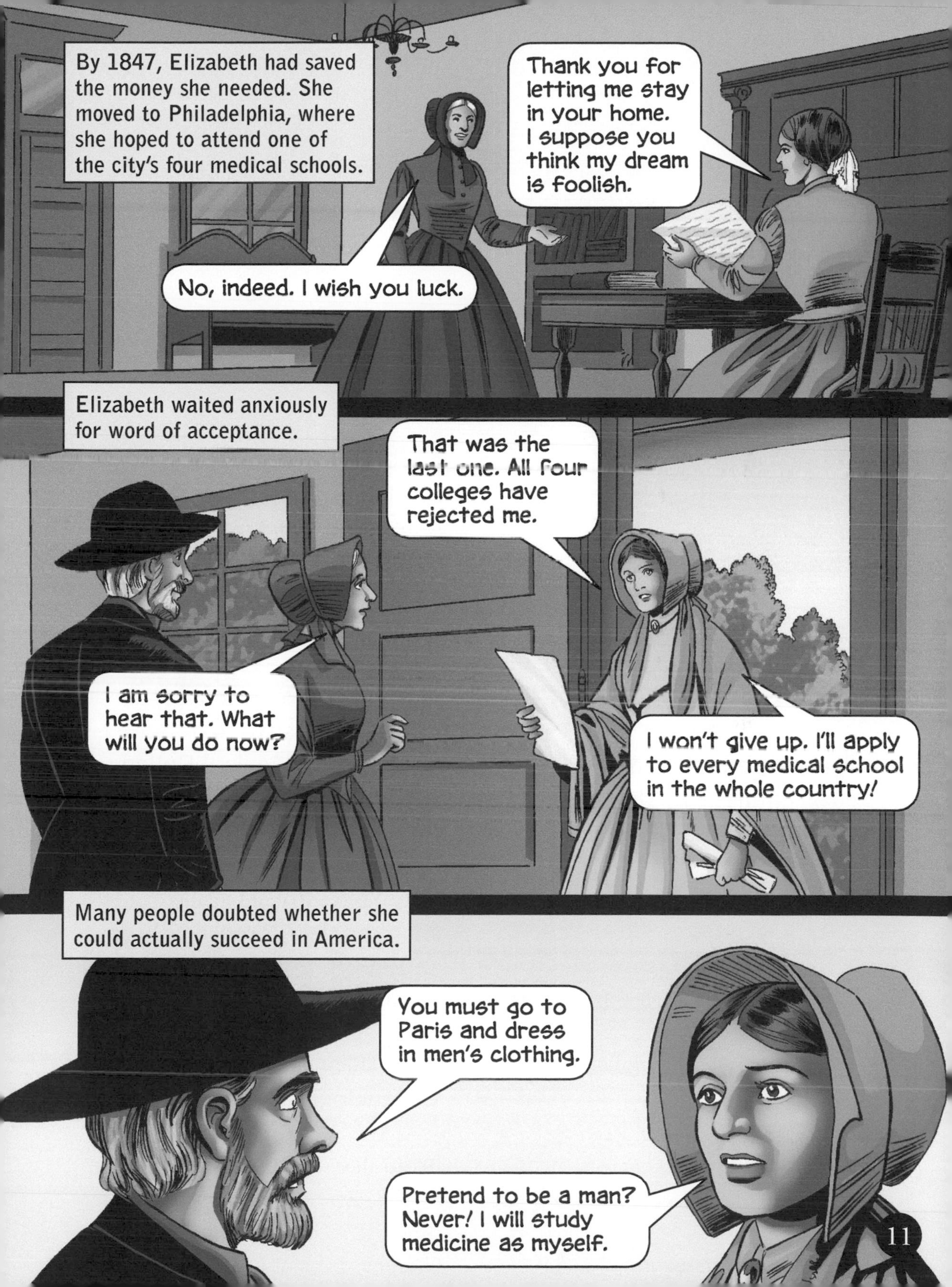
By 1847, Elizabeth had saved the money she needed. She moved to Philadelphia, where she hoped to attend one of the city's four medical schools.
Thank you for letting me stay in your home. I suppose you think my dream is foolish.
No, indeed. I wish you luck.
Elizabeth waited anxiously for word of acceptance.
That was the last one. All four colleges have rejected me.
I am sorry to hear that. What will you do now?
I won't give up. I'll apply to every medical school in the whole country!
Many people doubted whether she could actually succeed in America.
You must go to Paris and dress in men's clothing.
Pretend to be a man? Never! I will study medicine as myself.

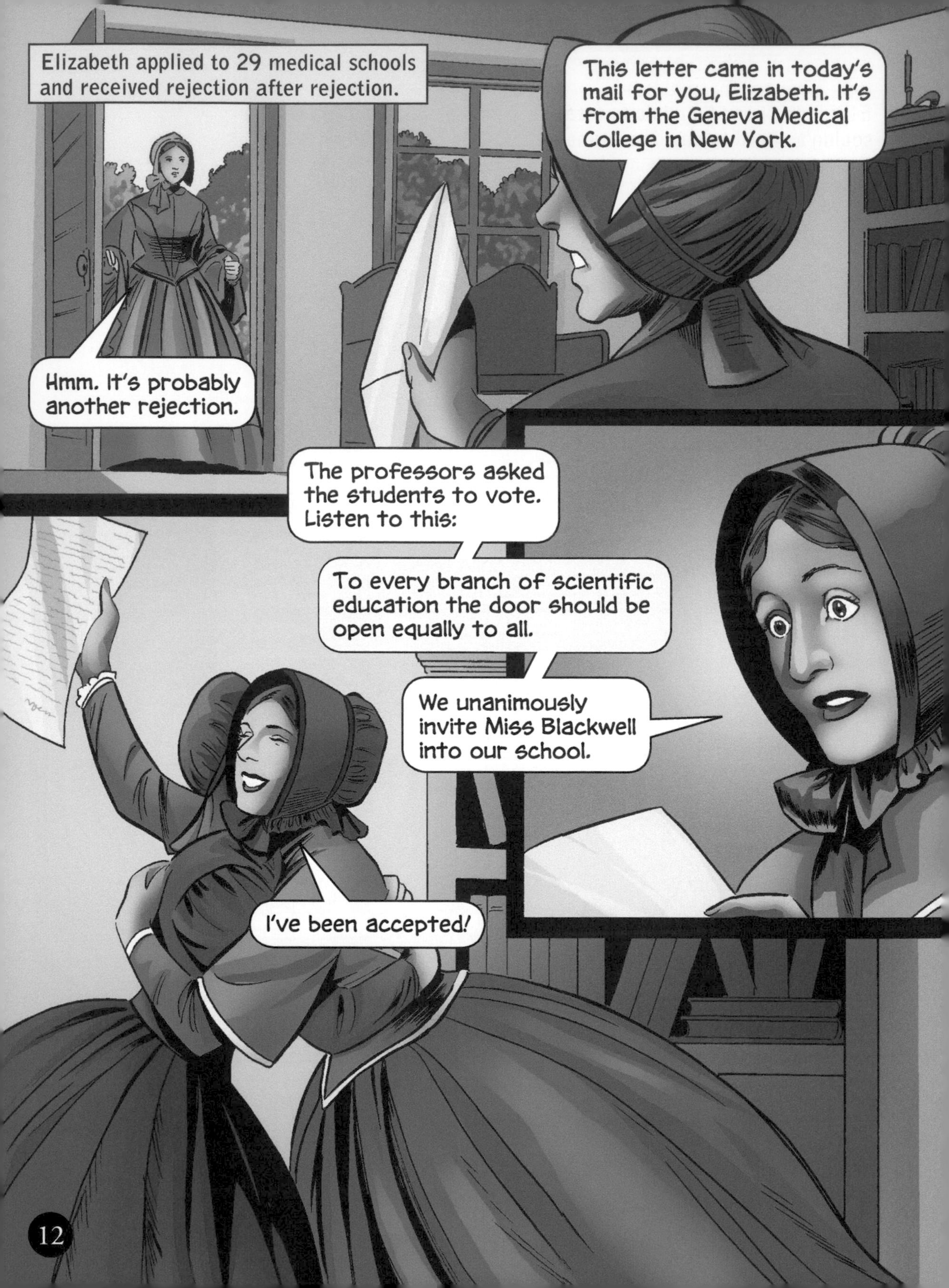
Elizabeth applied to 29 medical schools and received rejection after rejection.
This letter came in today's mail for you, Elizabeth. It's from the Geneva Medical College in New York.
Hmm. It's probably another rejection.
The professors asked the students to vote. Listen to this:
To every branch of scientific education the door should be open equally to all.
We unanimously invite Miss Blackwell into our school.
I've been accepted!

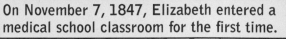

On November 7, 1847, Elizabeth entered a medical school classroom for the first time.

GENEVA
Medical College

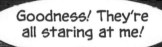

Goodness! They're all staring at me!

Well, I'm learning medicine. Let them stare if they want to.

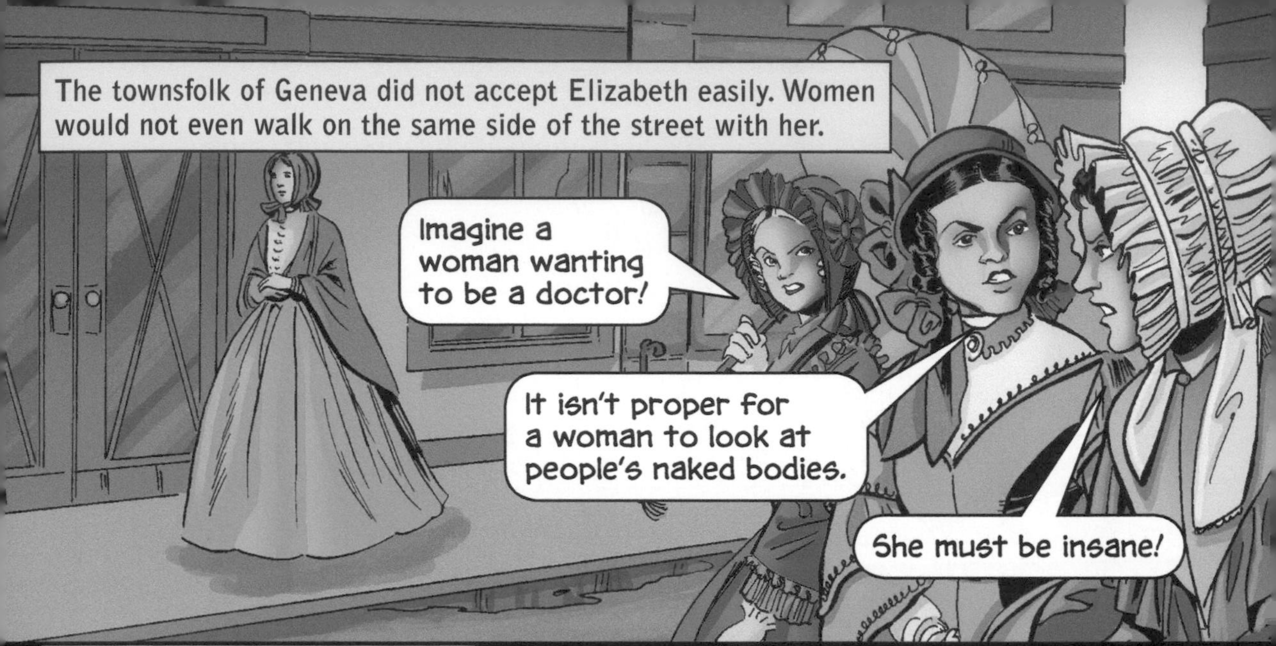
The townsfolk of Geneva did not accept Elizabeth easily. Women would not even walk on the same side of the street with her.
Imagine a woman wanting to be a doctor!
It isn't proper for a woman to look at people's naked bodies.
She must be insane!

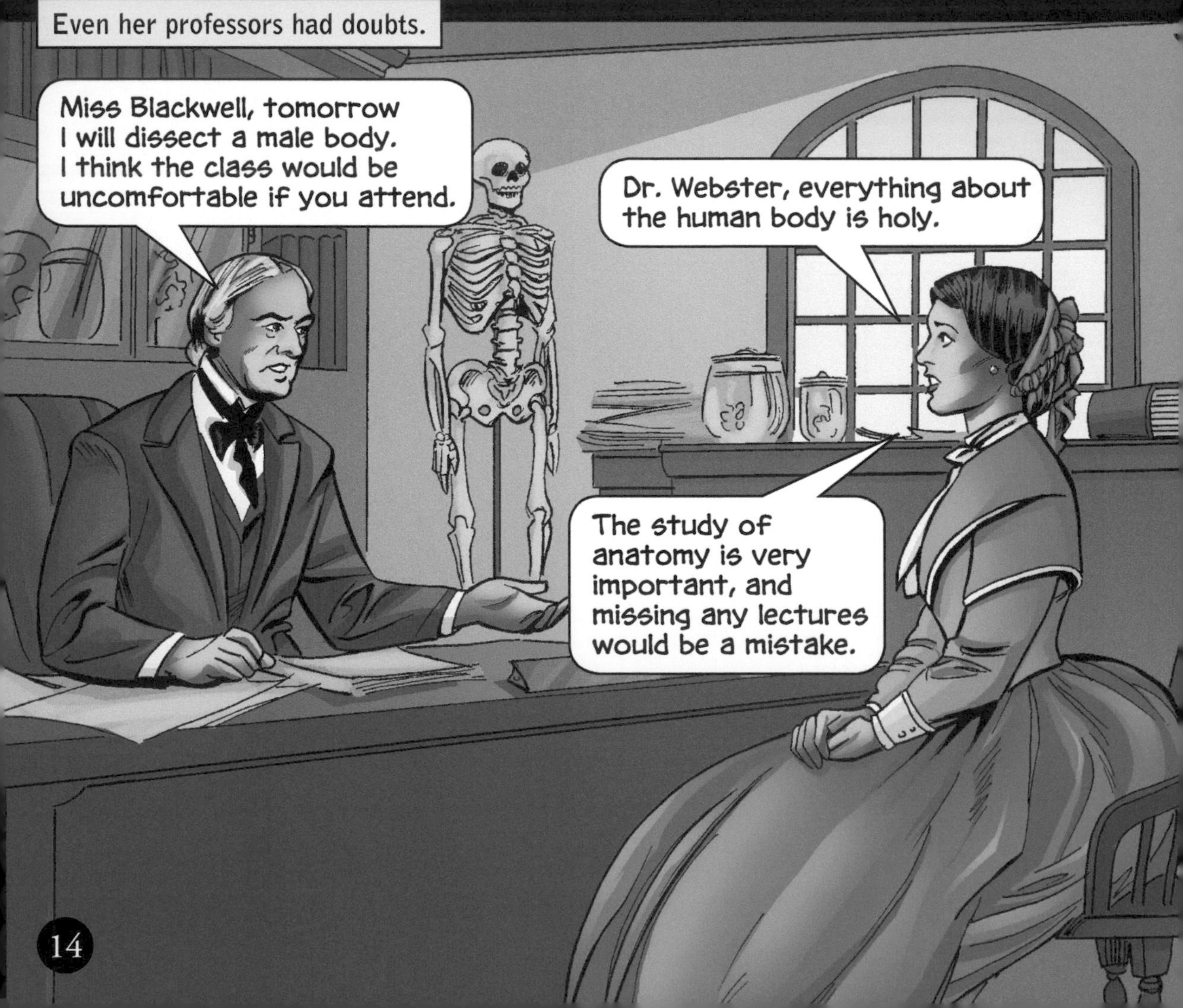
Even her professors had doubts.
Miss Blackwell, tomorrow I will dissect a male body. I think the class would be uncomfortable if you attend.
Dr. Webster, everything about the human body is holy.
The study of anatomy is very important, and missing any lectures would be a mistake.

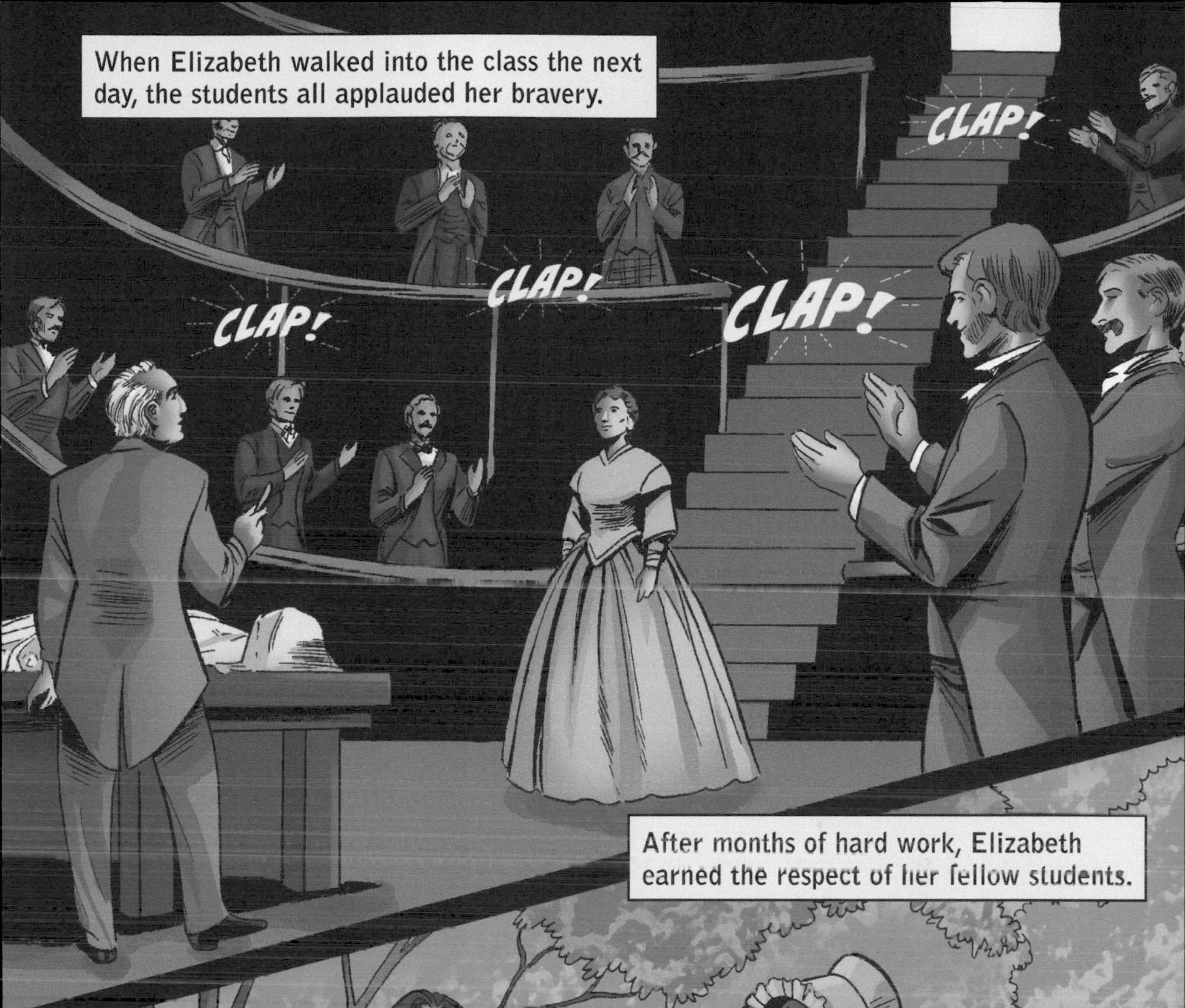
When Elizabeth walked into the class the next day, the students all applauded her bravery.
CLAP!
CLAP!
CLAP!
CLAP!
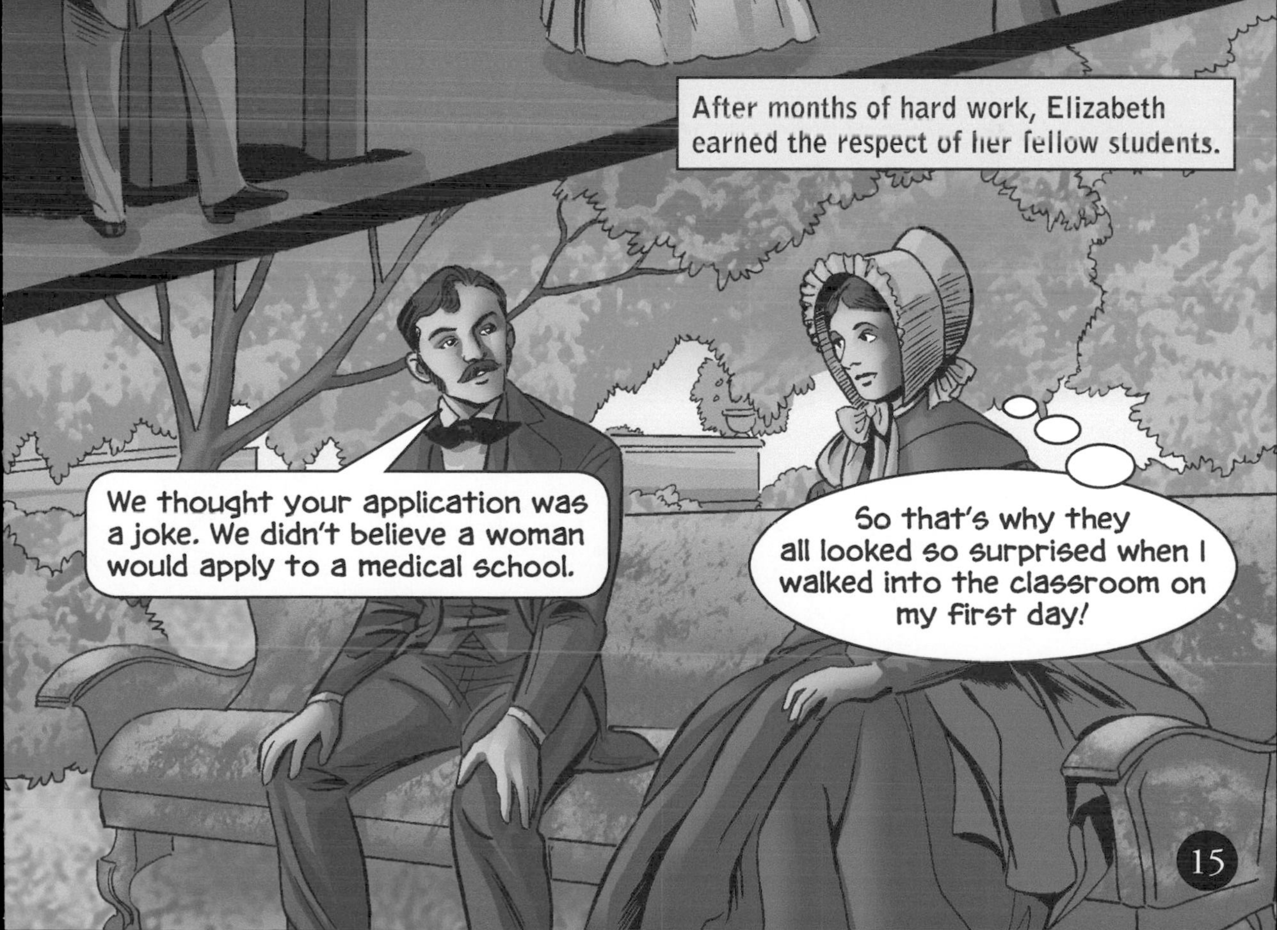
After months of hard work, Elizabeth earned the respect of her fellow students.
We thought your application was a joke. We didn't believe a woman would apply to a medical school.
So that's why they all looked so surprised when I walked into the classroom on my first day!

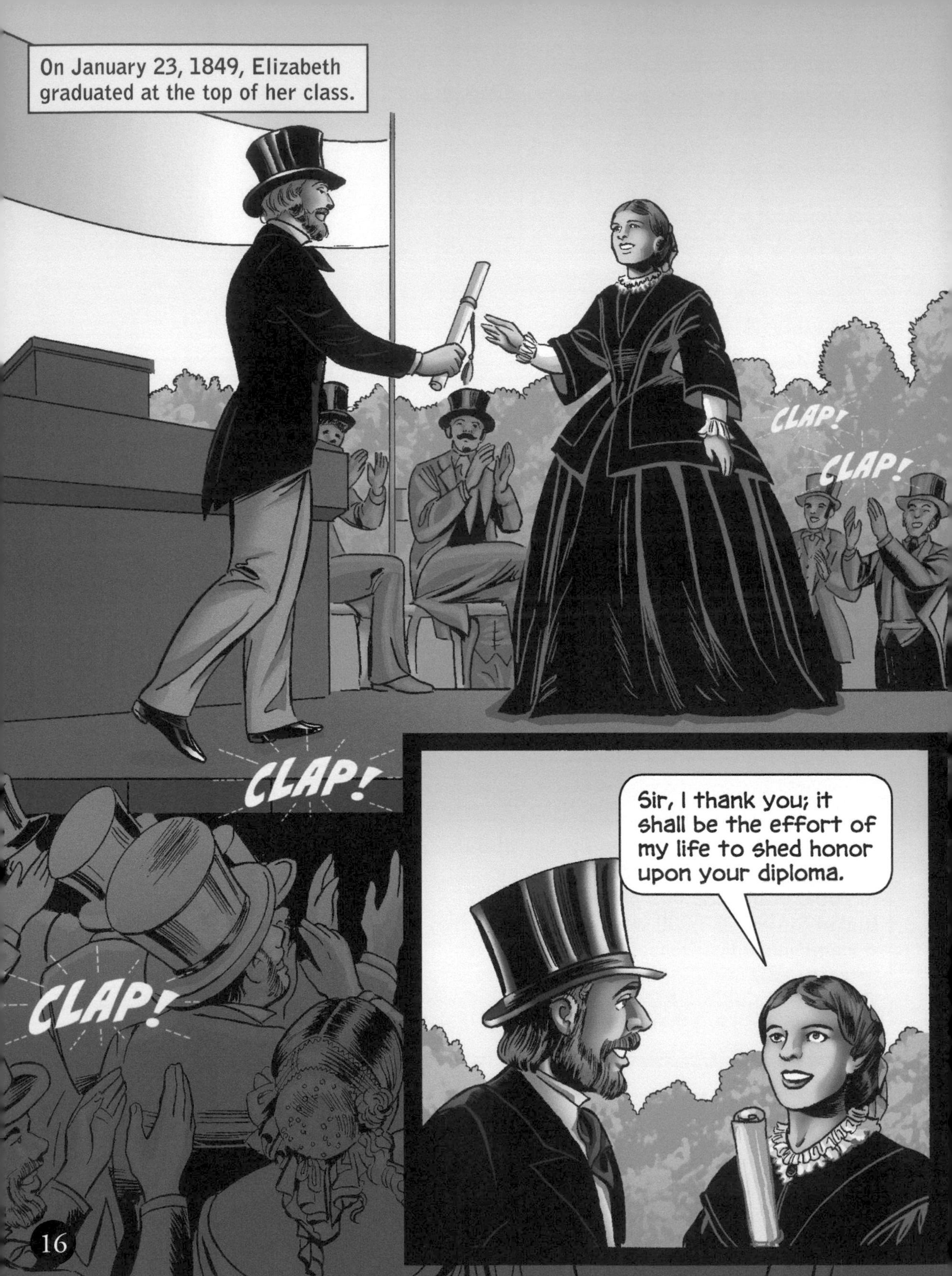
On January 23, 1849, Elizabeth graduated at the top of her class.
CLAP!
CLAP!
CLAP!
CLAP!
Sir, I thank you; it shall be the effort of my life to shed honor upon your diploma.

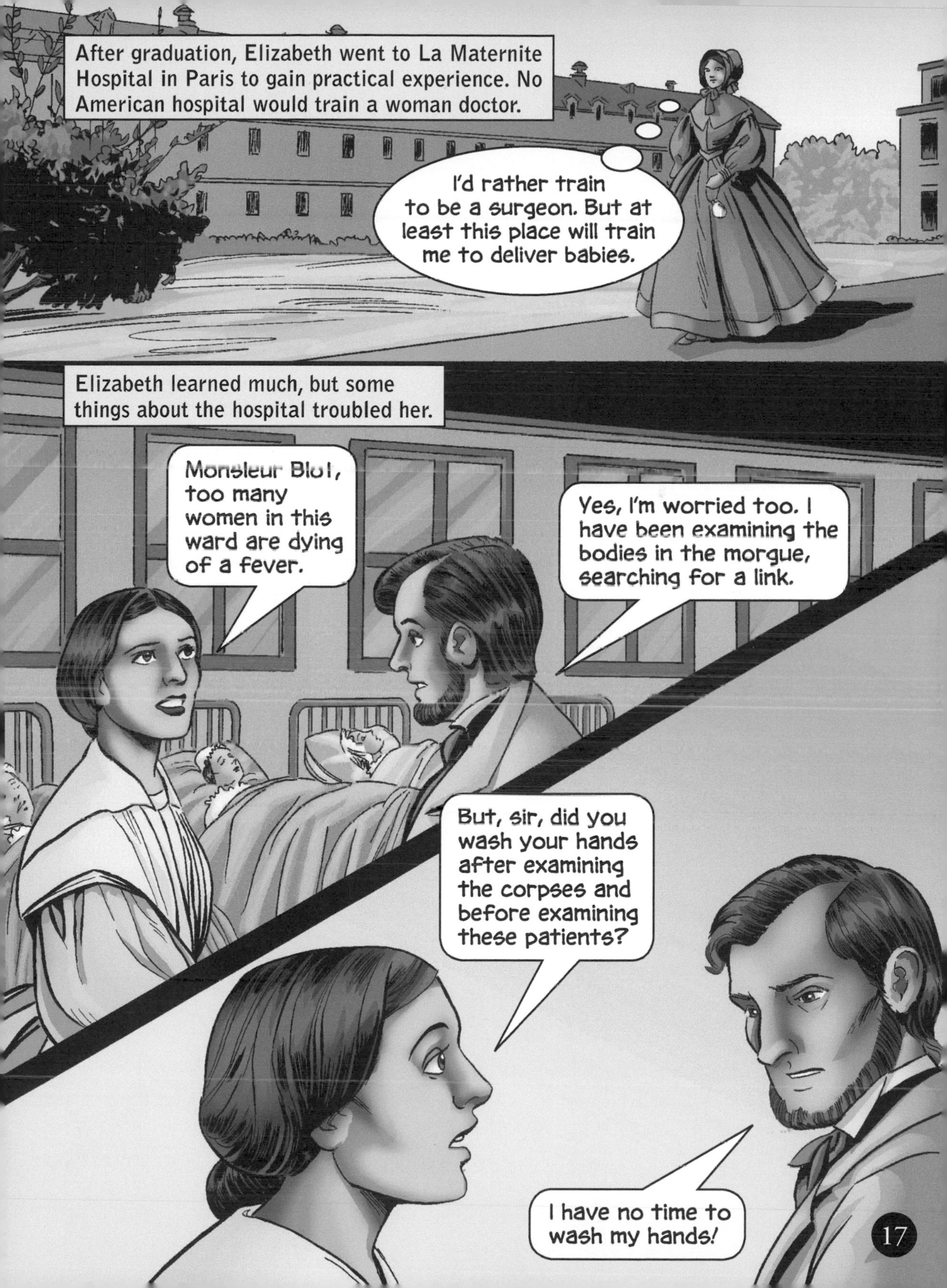

After graduation, Elizabeth went to La Maternite Hospital in Paris to gain practical experience. No American hospital would train a woman doctor.
I'd rather train to be a surgeon. But at least this place will train me to deliver babies.
Elizabeth learned much, but some things about the hospital troubled her.
Monsieur Blot, too many women in this ward are dying of a fever.
Yes, I'm worried too. I have been examining the bodies in the morgue, searching for a link.
But, sir, did you wash your hands after examining the corpses and before examining these patients?
I have no time to wash my hands!

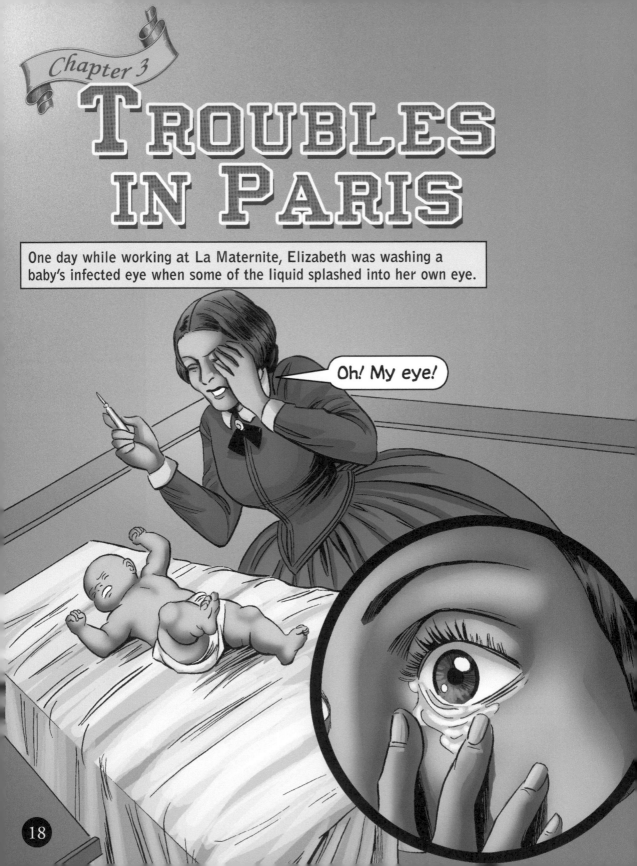

Chapter 3
TROUBLES IN PARIS

One day while working at La Maternite, Elizabeth was washing a baby's infected eye when some of the liquid splashed into her own eye.

Oh! My eye!

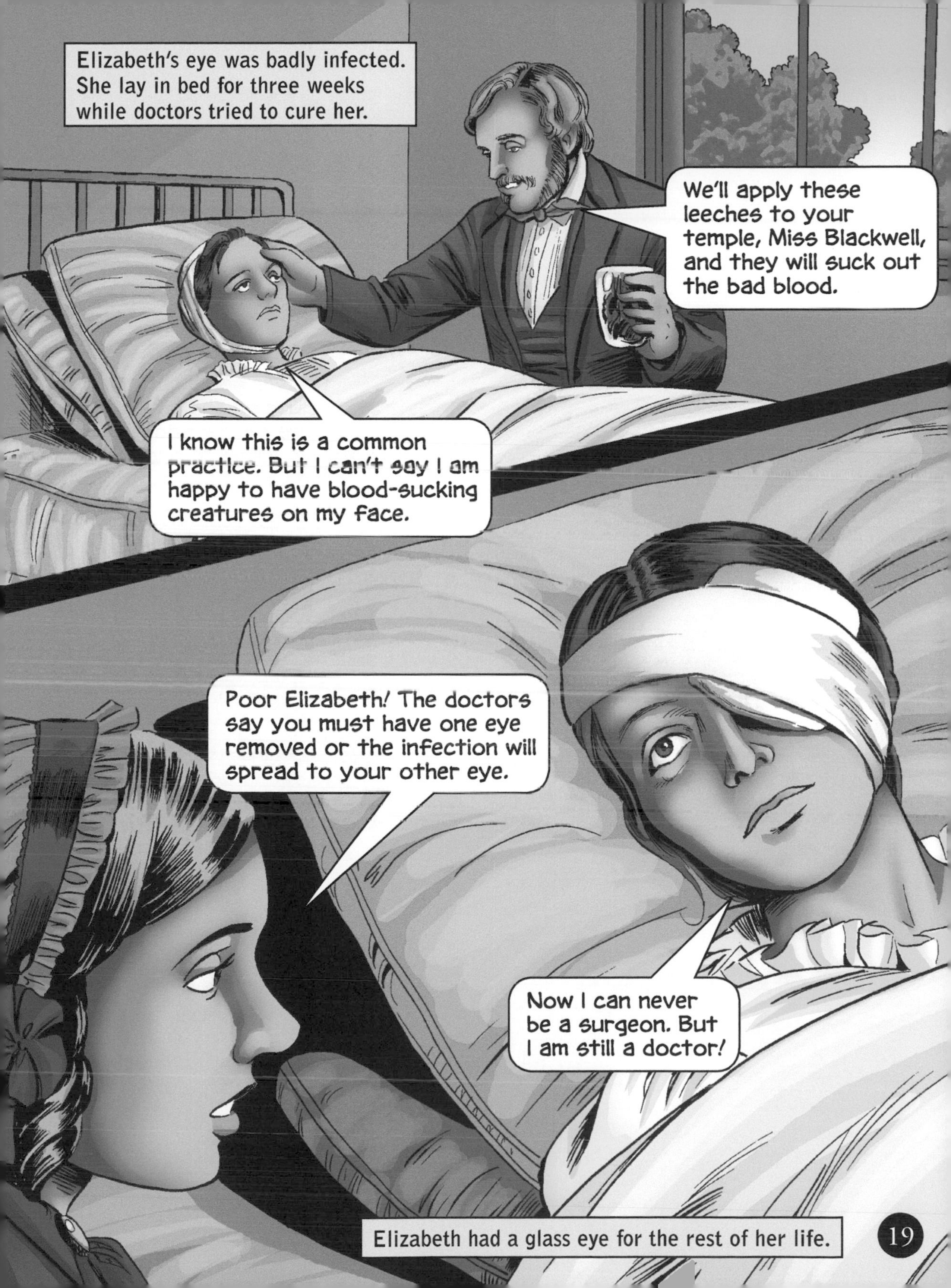
Elizabeth's eye was badly infected. She lay in bed for three weeks while doctors tried to cure her.
We'll apply these leeches to your temple, Miss Blackwell, and they will suck out the bad blood.
I know this is a common practice. But I can't say I am happy to have blood-sucking creatures on my face.
Poor Elizabeth! The doctors say you must have one eye removed or the infection will spread to your other eye.
Now I can never be a surgeon. But I am still a doctor!
Elizabeth had a glass eye for the rest of her life.

After she recovered, Elizabeth went to London to continue learning. She met Florence Nightingale, and they became great friends.
I want to become a nurse, but my parents don't approve. They say that hospitals are not a proper place for a lady.
Everyone said I would never be a doctor.

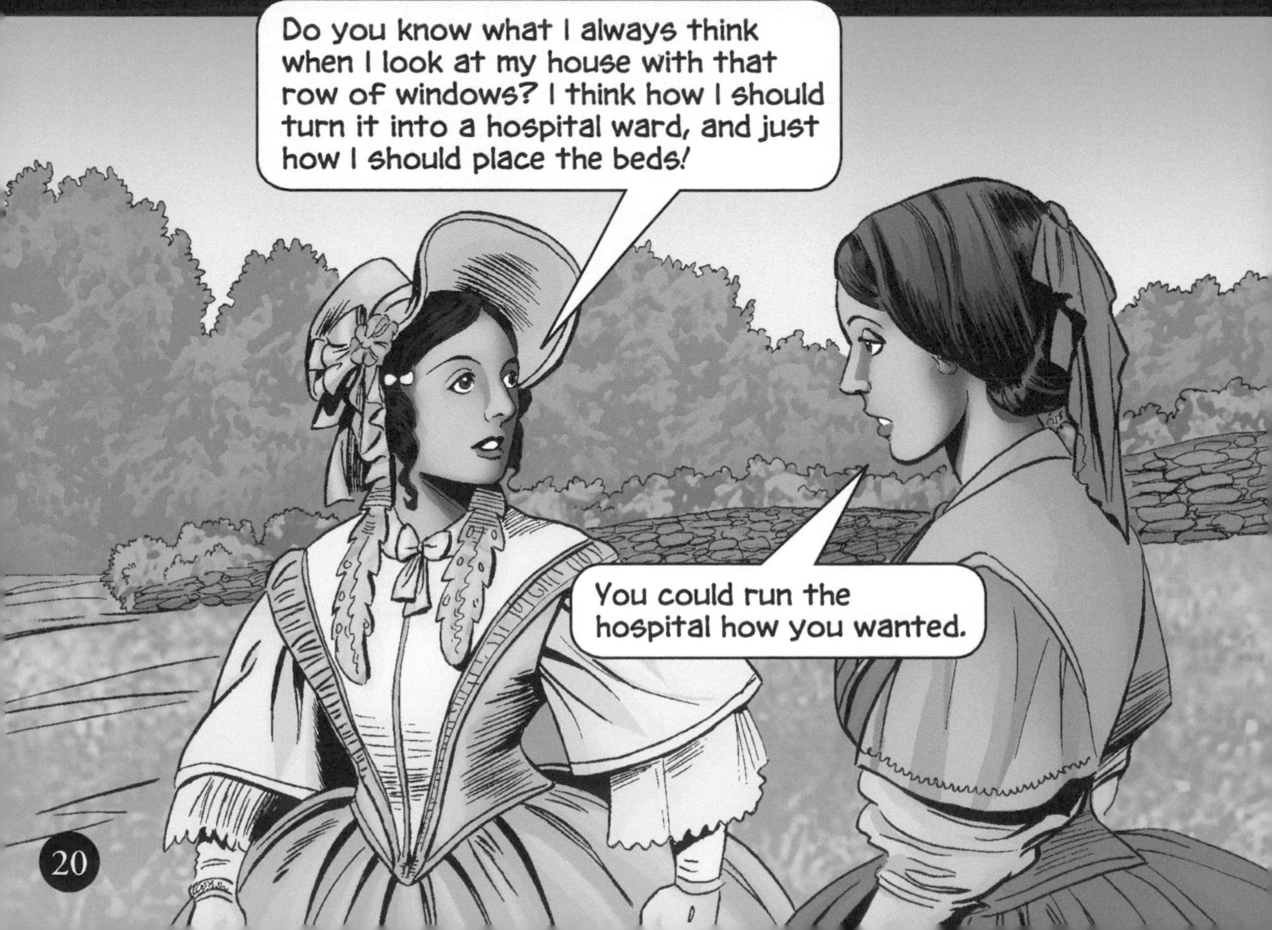
Do you know what I always think when I look at my house with that row of windows? I think how I should turn it into a hospital ward, and just how I should place the beds!
You could run the hospital how you wanted.

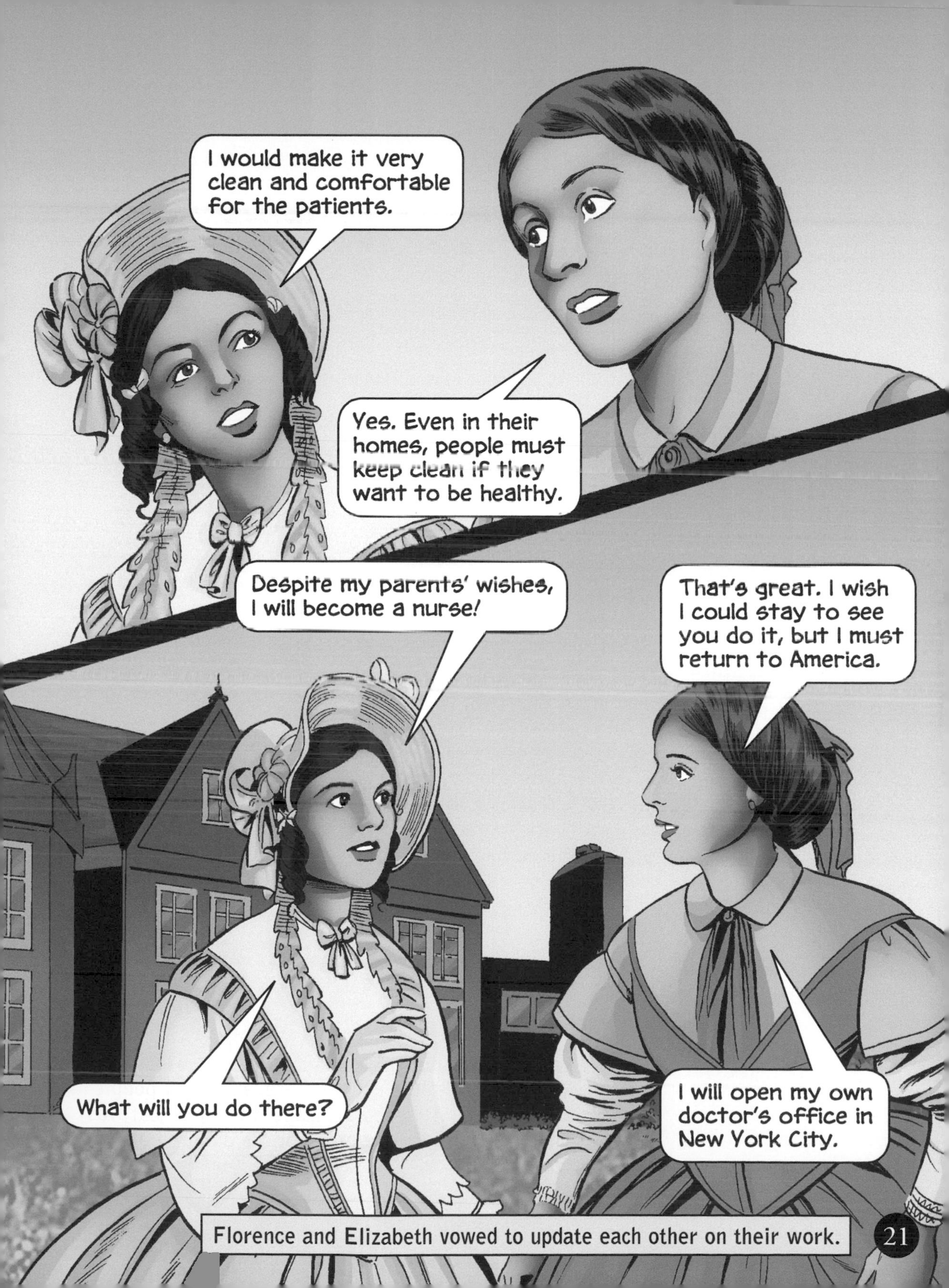
I would make it very clean and comfortable for the patients.
Yes. Even in their homes, people must keep clean if they want to be healthy.
Despite my parents' wishes, I will become a nurse!
That's great. I wish I could stay to see you do it, but I must return to America.
What will you do there?
I will open my own doctor's office in New York City.
Florence and Elizabeth vowed to update each other on their work.

Chapter 4

A Dream Comes True

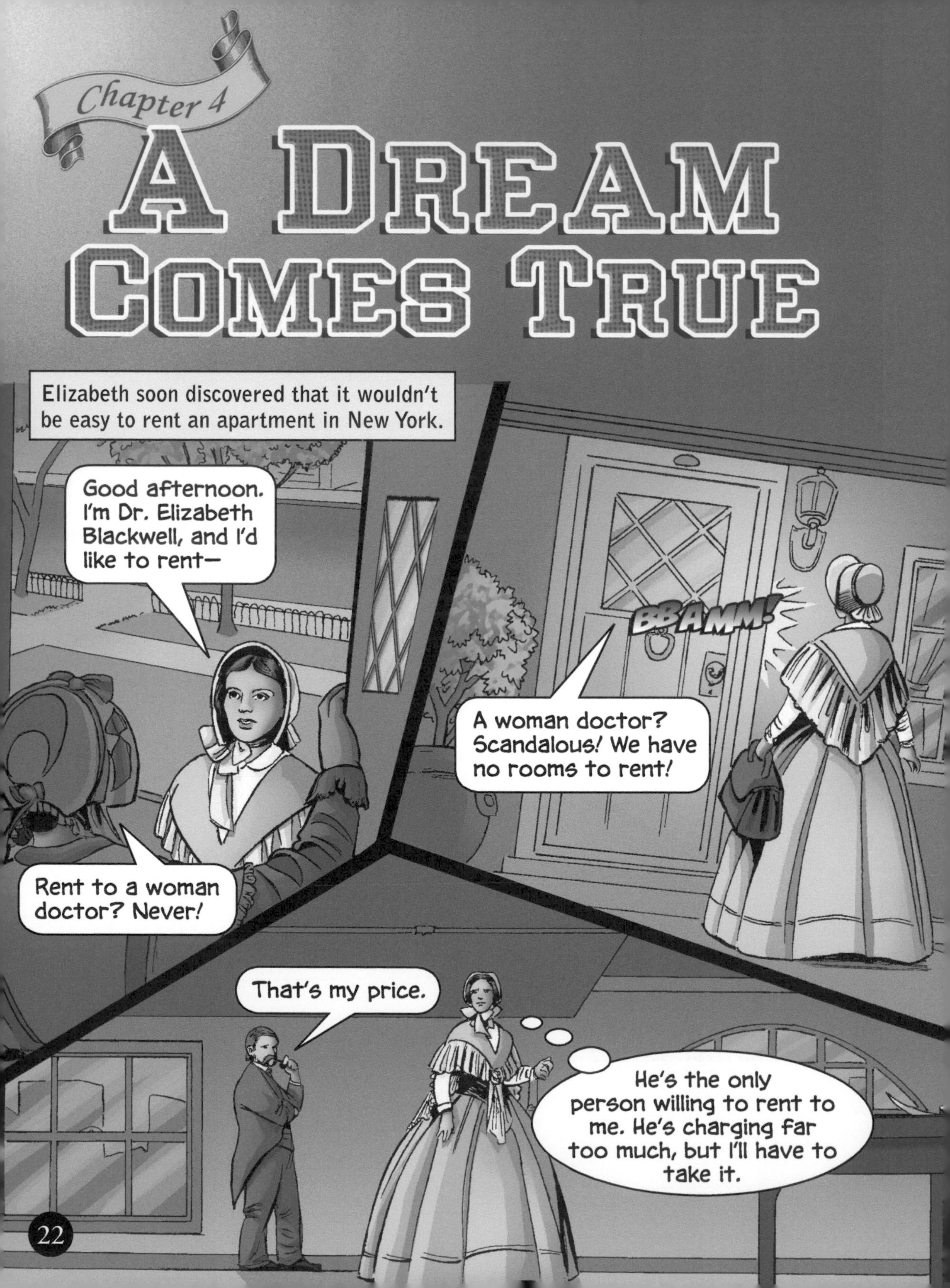

Elizabeth soon discovered that it wouldn't be easy to rent an apartment in New York.
Good afternoon. I'm Dr. Elizabeth Blackwell, and I'd like to rent—
Rent to a woman doctor? Never!
BBAMM!
A woman doctor? Scandalous! We have no rooms to rent!
That's my price.
He's the only person willing to rent to me. He's charging far too much, but I'll have to take it.

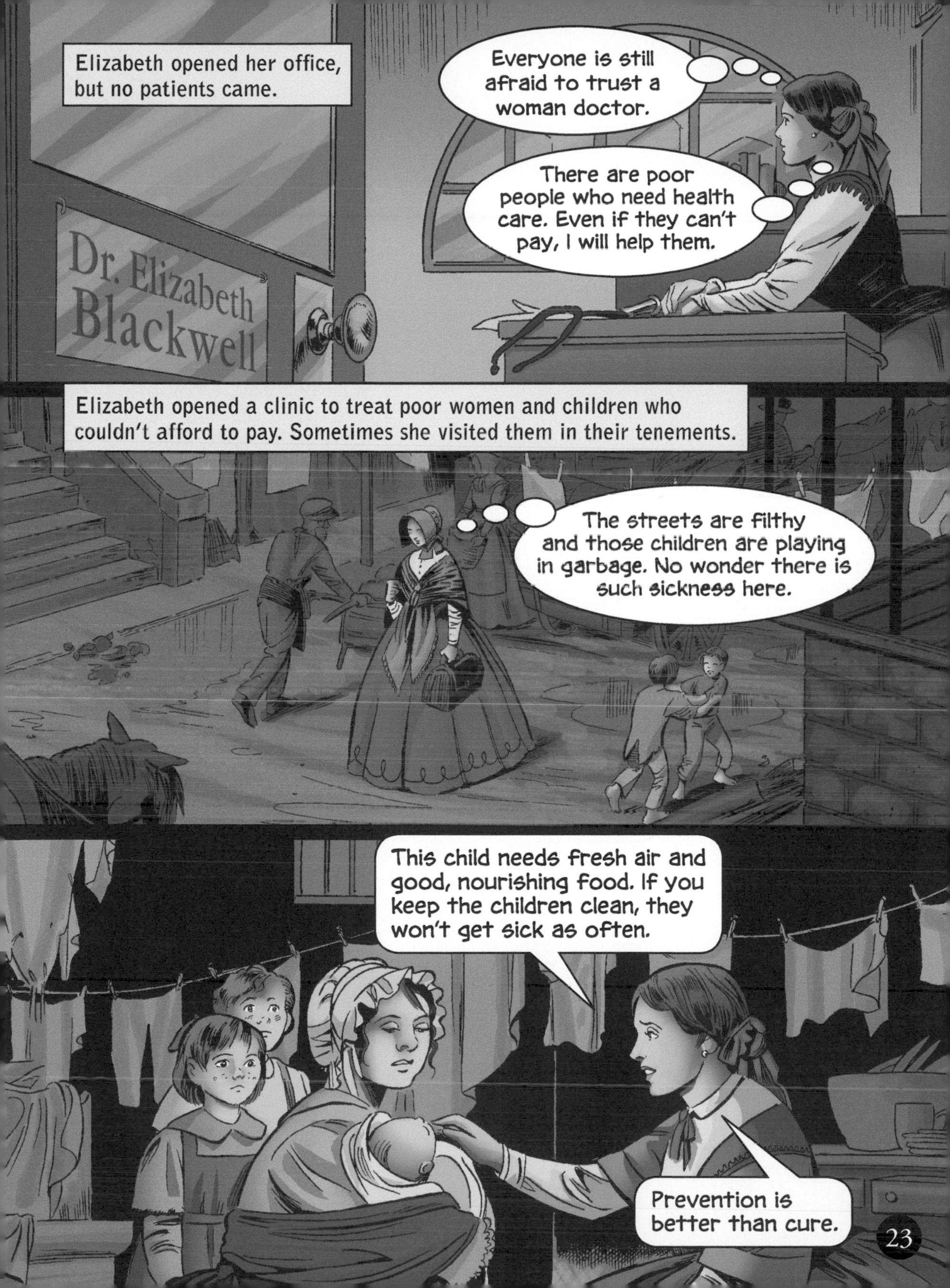

Elizabeth opened her office, but no patients came.
Everyone is still afraid to trust a woman doctor.
There are poor people who need health care. Even if they can't pay, I will help them.
Dr. Elizabeth Blackwell
Elizabeth opened a clinic to treat poor women and children who couldn't afford to pay. Sometimes she visited them in their tenements.
The streets are filthy and those children are playing in garbage. No wonder there is such sickness here.
This child needs fresh air and good, nourishing food. If you keep the children clean, they won't get sick as often.
Prevention is better than cure.

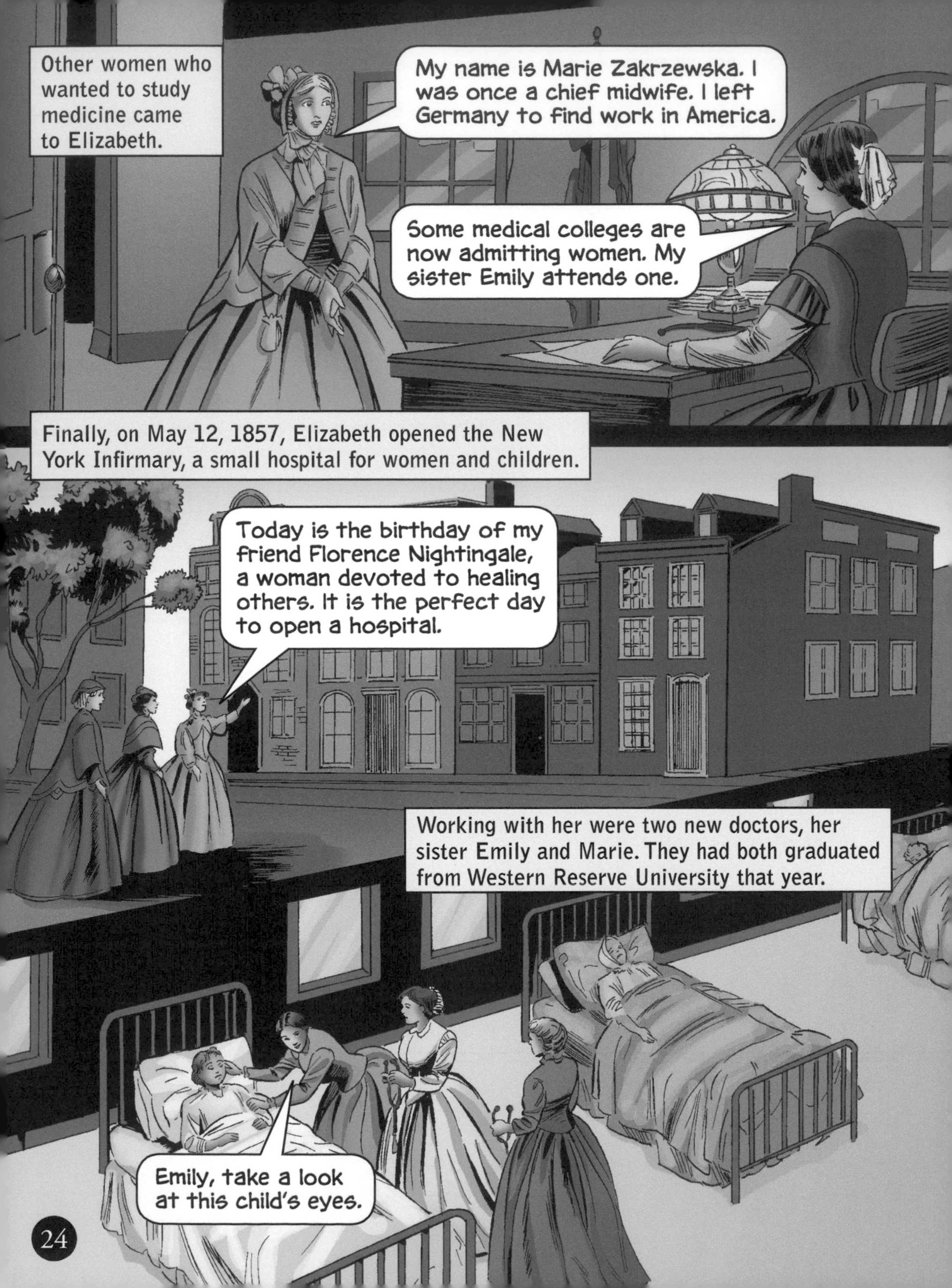
Other women who wanted to study medicine came to Elizabeth.
My name is Marie Zakrzewska. I was once a chief midwife. I left Germany to find work in America.
Some medical colleges are now admitting women. My sister Emily attends one.
Finally, on May 12, 1857, Elizabeth opened the New York Infirmary, a small hospital for women and children.
Today is the birthday of my friend Florence Nightingale, a woman devoted to healing others. It is the perfect day to open a hospital.
Working with her were two new doctors, her sister Emily and Marie. They had both graduated from Western Reserve University that year.
Emily, take a look at this child's eyes.

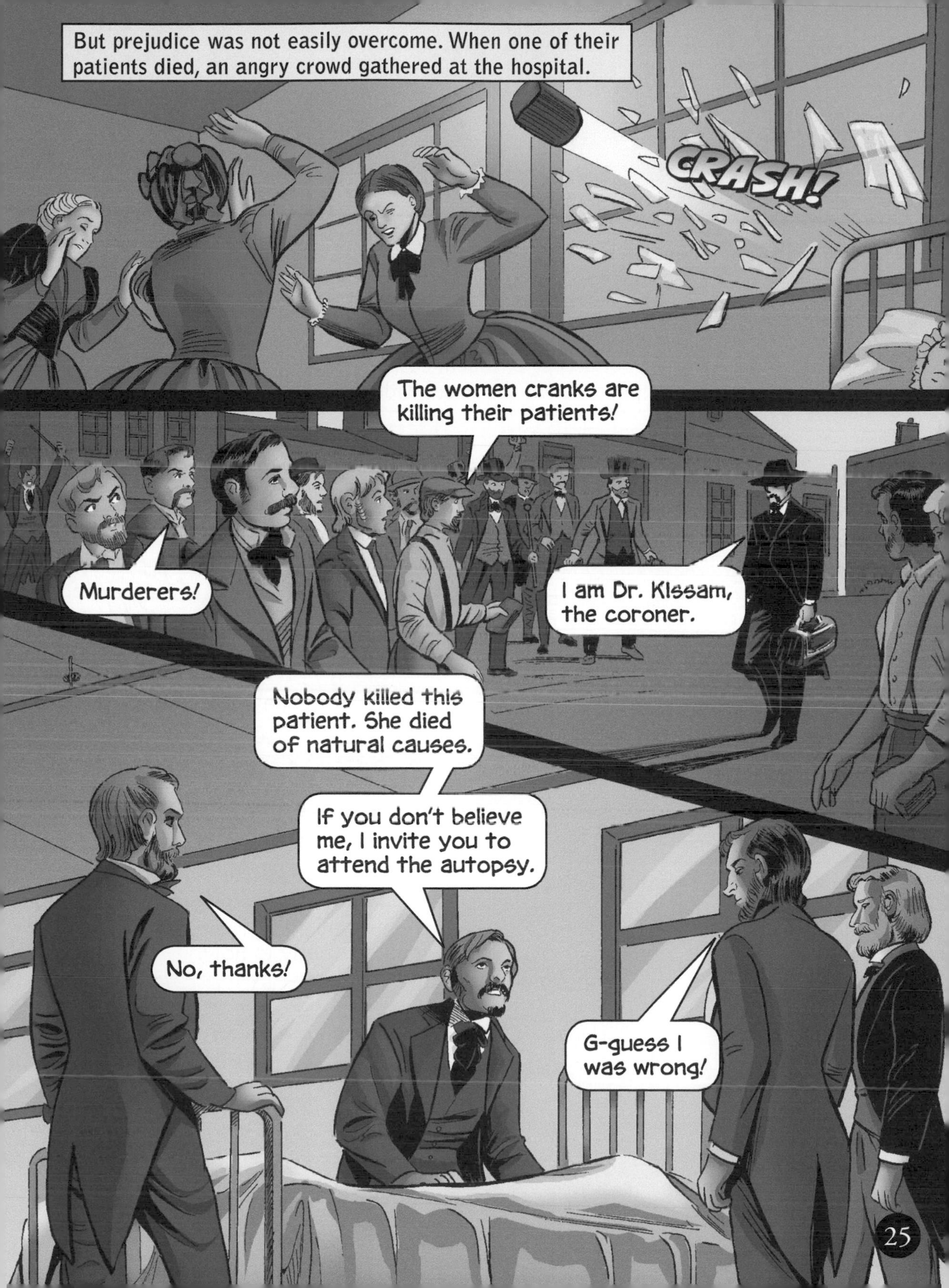
But prejudice was not easily overcome. When one of their patients died, an angry crowd gathered at the hospital.
CRASH!
The women cranks are killing their patients!
Murderers!
I am Dr. Kissam, the coroner.
Nobody killed this patient. She died of natural causes.
If you don't believe me, I invite you to attend the autopsy.
No, thanks!
G-guess I was wrong!

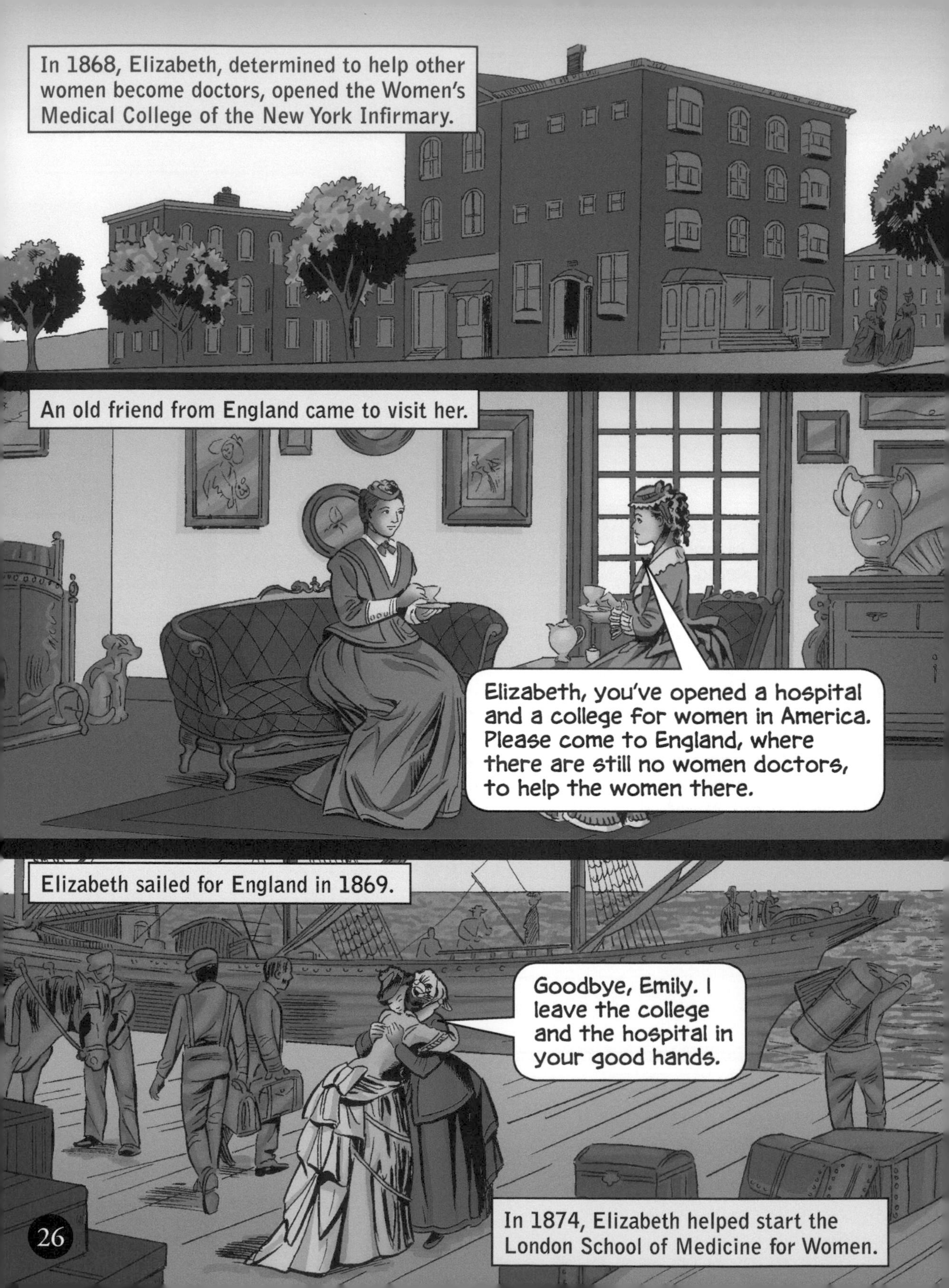
In 1868, Elizabeth, determined to help other women become doctors, opened the Women's Medical College of the New York Infirmary.
An old friend from England came to visit her.
Elizabeth, you've opened a hospital and a college for women in America. Please come to England, where there are still no women doctors, to help the women there.
Elizabeth sailed for England in 1869.
Goodbye, Emily. I leave the college and the hospital in your good hands.
In 1874, Elizabeth helped start the London School of Medicine for Women.

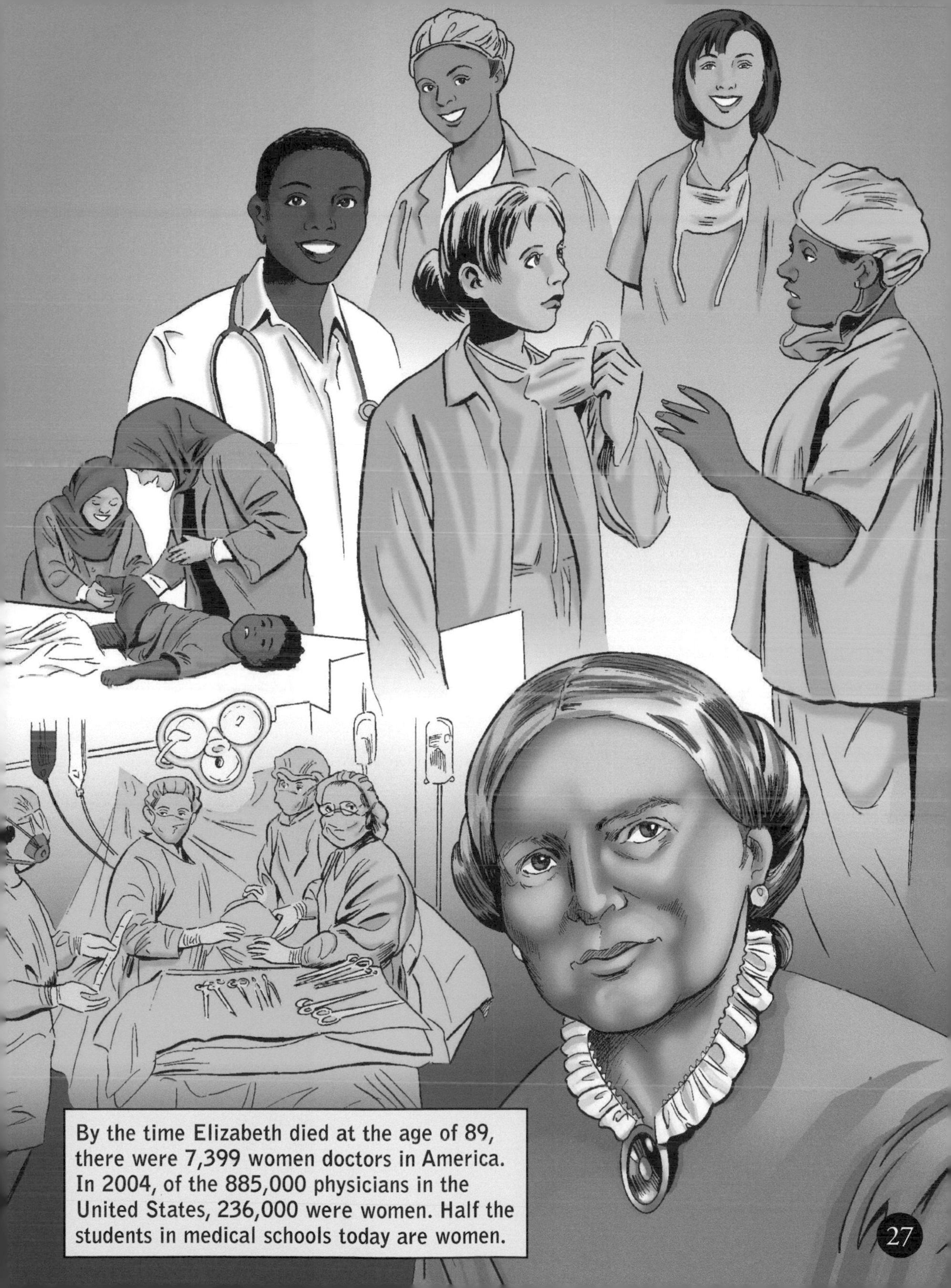
By the time Elizabeth died at the age of 89, there were 7,399 women doctors in America. In 2004, of the 885,000 physicians in the United States, 236,000 were women. Half the students in medical schools today are women.

More about ELIZABETH BLACKWELL

- Elizabeth Blackwell was born February 3, 1821, in Bristol, England. She died May 31, 1910, in Sussex, England.

- Elizabeth's friend Florence Nightingale did become a nurse. In 1854, Nightingale took 38 other nurses with her to work at the British Army hospitals during the Crimean War. She found filthy, unsanitary conditions, no medical supplies, and doctors who did not want to work with the women. Sometimes she worked as many as 20 hours a day to get the hospitals cleaned up. Her work made her world-famous. She later opened the Nightingale School for Nurses, the first school to offer professional training to nurses.

- Although Elizabeth never married, she wanted a family. In 1854, she adopted an Irish orphan, Kitty Barry.

- During the Civil War (1861–1865), Elizabeth and Emily Blackwell trained nurses to serve in Union army hospitals. The Superintendant of Female Nurses, with whom they worked, was a famous reformer named Dorothea Dix. Dix helped found 32 mental hospitals, 15 schools for people with special needs, a school for the blind, and many training schools for nurses.

- The Geneva Medical College, where Elizabeth graduated, is now the Hobart and William Smith Colleges. Since 1958, they have presented the Elizabeth Blackwell Award to outstanding women. The medal bears a portrait of Elizabeth and a quote from a letter she wrote at Geneva College in 1847: "I cannot but congratulate myself on having found at last the right place for my beginning."

- Many prominent women worked at the New York Infirmary, including Dr. Rebecca Cole, the second African-American woman doctor in the United States. In 1867, Cole received her medical degree from the Woman's Medical College of Pennsylvania. Elizabeth made Cole the hospital's health visitor. Cole visited poor slum families in their homes and taught them how to stay healthy.

- The New York Infirmary, the hospital that Elizabeth opened in 1857, still exists today as the New York University Downtown Hospital.

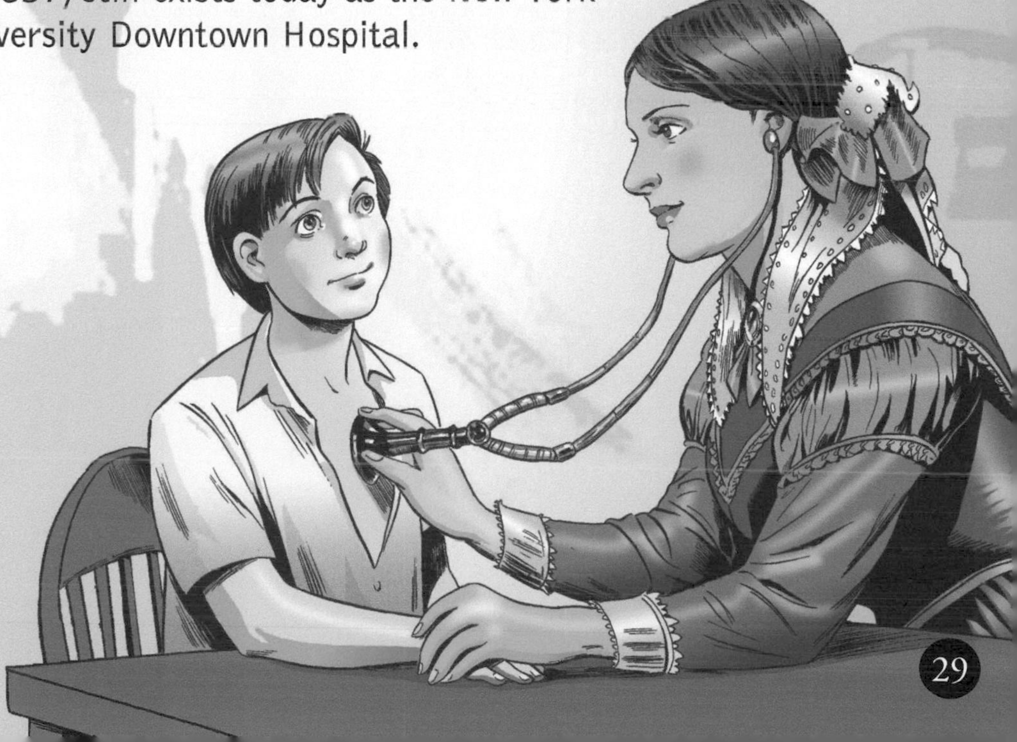

Glossary

autopsy (AW-top-see)—an examination performed on a dead person to find the cause of death

coroner (KOR-uh-ner)—a medical official who investigates deaths

crank (KRANGK)—someone with strange ideas

prejudice (PREJ-uh-diss)—an opinion formed without taking the time and care to judge fairly or without knowing all the facts

refinery (ri-FYE-nuh-ree)—a factory for purifying metal, sugar, or other things

tenement (TEN-uh-muhnt)—a run-down, crowded apartment building often found in a poor part of a city

unanimous (yoo-NAN-uh-muhss)—agreed on by everyone

unsanitary (un-SAN-uh-ter-ee)—dirty and unhealthy

Internet Sites

FactHound offers a safe, fun way to find Internet sites related to this book. All of the sites on FactHound have been researched by our staff.

Here's how:
1. Visit *www.facthound.com*
2. Choose your grade level.
3. Type in this book ID **0736864970** for age-appropriate sites. You may also browse subjects by clicking on letters, or by clicking on pictures and words.
4. Click on the **Fetch It** button.

FactHound will fetch the best sites for you!

Read More

Binns, Tristan Boyer. *Elizabeth Blackwell: First Woman Physician.* Great Life Stories. New York: Franklin Watts, 2005.

Kent, Deborah. *Elizabeth Blackwell: Physician and Health Educator.* Our People. Chanhassen, Minn.: Child's World, 2004.

Peck, Ira. *Elizabeth Blackwell: The First Woman Doctor.* A Gateway Biography. Brookfield, Conn.: Millbrook Press, 2000.

Bibliography

Blackwell, Elizabeth. *Pioneer Work in Opening the Medical Profession to Women.* Amherst, N.Y.: Humanity Books, 2005.

Clapp, Patricia. *Dr. Elizabeth: The Story of the First Woman Doctor.* New York: Lothrop, Lee & Shepard, 1974.

Glimm, Adele. *Elizabeth Blackwell: First Woman Doctor of Modern Times.* New York: McGraw-Hill, 2000.

Kline, Nancy. *Elizabeth Blackwell: A Doctor's Triumph.* Barnard Biography Series. Berkeley, Calif.: Conari Press, 1997.

Index